COLORS OF COURAGE: PAVING A PATH TO FREEDOM

Written By Jen Torres
Illustrated by Arefieva Anzhelika

eBook ISBN

979-8-9995922-1-7

979-8-9995922-3-1

Paperback ISBN

979-8-9995922-0-0

979-8-9995922-2-4

Hardback ISBN

979-8-9995922-4-8

979-8-9995922-5-5

Dedication

In memory of my abuela Icha, thanks for following your motherly instinct, your decision to get involved saved us. To my mom, thank you for not giving up and fighting as best you could.

Acknowledgment

First and foremost, I would like to thank God for being present in my life even when I did not notice it at the time. To my Abuela Icha, even though she is not physically here with us, I know when I am happy it is because her presence fills my heart with love and joy.

To my editor Gabriela Alvarado, thank you for steering me in the right direction, and putting up with this novice author. You are very skilled in the craft of writing, and I am glad you agreed to help me on this journey.

To the professional illustrator Arefieva Anzhelika, thank you for bringing my childhood story to life with your remarkable and creative artistry.

To my Beta readers, my bestie Vonnie and her daughter Adrianne thank you for reading my story and being honest with your critic. Vonnie thank you for listening to me for two years talking about this book, I probably drove you nuts talking about it. I truly appreciate you both.

Thank you, Ty, and Lucy, for praying for my wellbeing and success on this journey.

To my husband Hector and my sons Bebo, Alex and Bryan for being so supportive during my new adventure into the author world. To my family and friends thank you for being there for me in all the tough times in my life. Love you all so much.

To the readers, thank you for giving me the opportunity to become an Author, because without your support this book journey would not be possible.

Thank you to everyone involved in helping my dream of becoming an author a reality.

Finally, thank you mom for giving me your blessing to write this story. God has not forgotten you, and I have a feeling the best is yet to come.

About The Author

Jen Torres was born in Philadelphia, PA. She spent a portion of her early years between Puerto Rico and Springfield, Massachusetts. She spent the remainder of her youth in Villalba, Puerto Rico, where she finally learned to speak Spanish.

She is married and has a stepdaughter and three sons.

It wasn't until a year after her grandmother's passing in 2004 that she discovered her love for writing. The first short story she wrote is about her grandmother. She is now working on that story's completion.

Jen has survived Cancer twice. For this reason, she decided it was time for her story to be known.

She is not a victim; she is a survivor.

Work and raising a family took up much of her time, and she stopped writing for twenty years. She didn't decide to pick up writing again until her boys were all grown and no longer in need of her care.

Her hobby is crafting with epoxy/uv resin. She is a movie buff; her favorite genres are Romantic comedies, Action, Fantasy and Paranormal movies. Christmas movies are by far her favorite.

She loves reading Devotions to start her day.

Favorite Romance book is the "Note Book."

If you would like to follow her on this journey you can find her on:

Facebook: Jen Torres – "Author"

Instagram: Jen Torres (New Author)

Email address: jentorresauthor@gmail.com

Author's Notes

The occurrences I wrote about in this book happened when I was a little girl, at the time when I was supposed to have a happy and fulfilling childhood experience.

Due to protecting the privacy of some individuals in my story, I do not mention their names. There is some that should be mentioned but I will not give them the gratification of feeling dominant or having a sense of accomplishment in their wrong doings.

I had to unearth these unpleasant memories to write about a time when survival was all we knew. It left a scar in my life and left my mother scrambling to pick up the pieces of what we thought would be broken forever.

In no manner do I think I am an expert about Domestic Violence; however, I lived it, and I am living proof that we can heal and there is a safe and normal life left to live after.

TABLE OF CONTENTS

Introduction

"To forgive and forget," that is what I tell myself to try and do almost every day of my life. I ask myself: can my mom possibly forgive the man who ruined her chances of living a normal life?

Can my mom forget those acts of intimidation and violence she endured for 6 years?

The answer to those questions is quite simple for a woman who has been down on her luck ever since and who never trusted a man to love her again.

Let's ask ourselves: what happens when children are involved and experience chaos during their young years?

Society had failed us; we were left to fend for ourselves. But did we ever really overcome all the injustice that was done to us?

I knew that asking my mom to unlock those horrible memories did not feel right, or fair, of me to do. I decided I would unlock those horrendous memories I had hidden in the vault deep within my own memory.

I am taking the chance to do this because I know that I am strong enough to be able to share my story, to possibly help someone else know and understand that they are *not* alone.

I am proof that when we fight through the obstacles, we can accomplish anything in life.

I, as a wife, a mother, and a friend can now exhale and feel blessed to have been given the chance to write my testimony.

Writing about this experience is meant to help others become aware of what the inside of an abusive home looks like and possibly help them realize that abuse of any kind is not OK; we must fight 'till the end and not lose hope.

Chapter 1: Discoveries

As children, we are only beginning to discover our individual self. Is there a way we can possibly understand all the ins and outs of life at such an early age? We depend on our parents to prepare us for everything life throws at us.

We are taught to be independent, responsible, and caring amongst other things we need to learn to be decent humans. What about being brave or strong, can that be taught or is it a learned behavior?

Only beginning our lives, unable to understand life and incapable of making our own decisions... what happens when it is tarnished by horrible occurrences?

All we can do is depend on our parents to help us get out of it and make the right decision for us. As a parent myself, I always worried about making a wrong decision that would affect my children's lives. Questioning my own decisions, whether they were right or wrong, helped me learn what was right for them.

One thing I will say is: parents are not perfect. There can be instances in an overly complex relationship where parents can become oblivious to the damage that a wrong decision can make for their children and how it can be momentous in the future.

When domestic abuse is involved, the damage becomes so severe it can change a child's way of seeing things for the rest of their lives, in turn causing their way of life to become a fight for survival.

Throughout the decades, women have evolved to be fighters, and we understand that it is unacceptable to be treated in such cruel manners – I say evolved because for most of us it had to be learned the hard way.

As someone who was subjected to domestic abuse as a child, I did not grow up to be a monster as some might expect. But one thing I did learn to be out of everything I endured is not a victim, but a *survivor*.

I always wondered if we would ever get away from the chaos. Was there ever going to be a moment when life was going to be kind to us? Would we stop feeling that heaviness on our chest and breathe anew? Most importantly will we ever not be afraid and be brave?

After experiencing violence the way we did, you learn to be extra cautious in life with every decision you make.

As children, we were forced to adapt to the atmosphere surrounding us, even if it was an unsafe one.

Chapter 2: Thoughts

I was between the ages of 4 and 9 when I had my life turned upside-down by a man whose sole purpose in life was to physically and mentally abuse my mother, my sister Aria and myself. I have four sisters on my mother's side, but only my first youngest sister and I experienced abuse.

Not quite sure if my sister remembers anything, but I sure do; I remember it all. It's imprinted in my brain, and I could never get rid of it, all I could do was hide it away somewhere deep in my memories.

It's hard to let go of the memories, eventually I learned to have control over what I wanted to remember and what I didn't.

I live a normal life now, and normal for me is the opposite of what I, and my family, experienced. Normal for me is being able to speak my mind and not feel threatened. Normal is being able to breathe and not be scared to go out and experience the world. Normal is feeling love in every corner of my home.

I always promised myself I was not going to have the same life my mother had back then. Even though she tried to protect us as best she could, at the end of the day the damage was already done. Do not get me wrong, I am grateful to my mother, she took the brunt of it all; could things have been done differently, I don't think so. I think it was difficult for any of it to have been any different, because the fear had set in, and it was there to stay.

I ended up learning the hard way that some situations could not be fixed without having faith in life.

As a child, I imagined a different world, an unlikely existence, a place where I felt loved. I knew it was unrealistic, but just the thought of it being real made me feel safe and there was nothing I wanted more.

Chapter 3: The Beginning

Things were different in Springfield, MA in the 80's (well at least for us they were). It seemed as if people were just in denial of their surroundings, or maybe they chose to play ignorant to their surroundings.

Mom reached out for help so many times, but no one was willing to help. I am not sure if it was because of the language barrier, or people were simply scared to intervene. Even though she didn't speak English, she did understand it, and she always had me to interpret for her.

Let me take you back to when I was born. That momentous time when my mom and father became parents for the first time. My biological father was so ecstatic, so happy to become a dad that he showed me off any chance he got. My mom was happy as well, she had a baby girl with green eyes, such a pretty baby face—what more could she want.

I was nine months old when my biological father decided he wanted nothing to do with my mom. My parents were not married, they decided to move in together and once my mom became pregnant everything was great… until it wasn't.

As months went by, Mom started noticing that my father was showing less and less affection every day. He would stay out late, act weird, and pick fights with her. She knew something was up with this new behavior. Once my mom discovered he was seeing another woman, she packed up and left, without saying a word to him.

The betrayal my mom felt, a single mother, with a nine-month-old baby. She was on her own and could not help feeling unloved and unwanted when she found out about the affair. She did not have any other choice but to move back to Puerto Rico with my grandparents.

To my understanding—and this is coming directly from my biological father's mouth—he did not love my mom anymore, and he had feelings for another woman (cruel, right?). My mom never really spoke about it, which is why I asked him, despite it being a slap in the face.

She was welcomed back home with open arms, baby and all, no questions asked. My mother spent the first three years of my life in Villalba, PR, in the mountains with my abuelos (grandparents). I was nicknamed *Palomita Blanca* because of my pale complexion.

There, my mom felt safe and loved. My grandparents loved having a baby in the house again. My mom is one of the youngest of the eight children; my abuelos had a very big family—four boys and four girls.

They all helped each other out and looked out for us. The few years we were there, my mom got a lot of help from the family, but she eventually decided it was time to branch out again and see what else life had in store for us.

Mom had an older sister that was married, had five sons and lived in Springfield, MA. She decided we'd move in with them for some months until they helped her find an apartment of her own. My uncles also decided to leave home (Puerto Rico) and venture to Springfield. There they all found jobs at this tobacco field, including my mom.

Though everything was going great, it got hard after my mom started to realize she was on her own with a child.

After a while, even though Mom worked, it was getting difficult for her financially. She realized there was no other choice but to move back in with my aunt again until she figured out what to do.

In the tobacco field, the men worked on one side of the field collecting tobacco leaves, while the women worked inside the building finishing the process.

There at that the field, Mom met the man that was going to become the biggest nightmare for us; the man who was going to change our lives forever.

That moment that would turn our lives into this endless spiral of uncertainty, and chaos was closing in and about to shape itself.

My mom, unaware of what the future would hold for us, fell in love and decided to move in with that man; (let's refer to him as an ogre for the sake of not giving him the power of speaking his name). I always wondered if it was out of necessity or fear of being alone that caused her to make that decision—being a single mom and having no one to really be with her while she raised her daughter.

We spent the following six years living in a nightmare that she couldn't seem to get away from. No matter how hard my mom tried, nothing was working for us.

Back then women always were taught they needed a man in order to survive in life.

We lived in an apartment building on Montmorenci Street. There were at least four floors of apartments on both sides and there was a stairway in the middle of the building. From what I can remember, we lived on the third floor. I saw the apartment building as a castle, guarded by an ogre who was purely evil and manipulated everyone to do his bidding.

My imagination was incredibly significant to me; it was my escape from the reality of my life.

After some time passed, my mom became pregnant with my first little sister Aria. At the beginning, there were some good moments; the excitement of having a baby sister, lots of toys, laughter and family memories.

However, it was like a dark cloud placed itself over the apartment building and with it came pain and fear. Not sure exactly when everything went downhill for us, but I realized soon our situation had changed from laughter and happiness, to cries and screams nearly every day.

I was between four and five years old when I started hearing someone weeping in the middle of the night and it was not my baby sister doing the crying. I also noticed the ogre's facial expressions had completely changed from normal to angry ones. He was constantly screaming at us; everything bothered him.

Things were not the same and our surroundings were changing for the worse.

Chapter 4: Rude Awakening

My mother had to stop working once she moved in with the ogre. He continued to work in the tobacco field, as a supervisor. He drove a blue bus so massive it could knock down the streetlights when it turned. It was painted a kind of blue you could see from a mile away.

He was in charge of picking up other employees to go work at the field. It became a daily routine for mom to sit by the window to watch him leave and return home. At the time, I did not think anything of it, I did not know there was a reason for this pattern.

Like many women back in the day, and like many other expectations out of women, she was brought up thinking women are meant to serve their man and do as they were told.

She grew up on those beliefs where the women were raised having to tend to a man's every need, maintain the home, and make sure they had those babies to keep the lineage going. Some were taught to believe women had no right to have their own opinion and had to agree with everything the husband said.

It's amazing how times have changed, and I am so glad they did. We women can speak our minds; we can be whatever we want to be. Are we still judged, do people still doubt us? Of course, but we don't care. Women thrive on proving others wrong. We have rights and we need to understand once and for all it is *NOT* ok to experience any kind of abuse.

I wouldn't wish it on anyone, not even the person I despise the most—to go through what we went through.

I remember my mom having a routine for certain things. I noticed if she forgot to complete any routines for the day, she would panic, and I couldn't understand why. If she heard a door closing, she would flinch at the noise it made, expecting it to be the ogre walking through it.

My sister Aria and I were not allowed to play in our rooms during the day, we could play in any other part of the apartment just not our own room. What a strange rule to set for children in their own home… We could only go into our room for bedtime, and mom had to make sure we were tucked in before she left the room.

I wondered why, but as a kid it really didn't matter as long as I had my toys. I was a big fan of Raggedy Ann dolls. My doll became my crying pillow during those years; her name was Mary.

At the age of five my mom had a friend who would come over to our apartment and teach me how to write my name, numbers, shapes, etc., by the time I started Kindergarten.

Hard to believe, I knew how to write my name in cursive at that age. That lady was Mom's only friend; I don't recall my mother talking to anyone else while she was with ogre.

She wouldn't even talk to the neighbors; she was not allowed to. Sounds crazy right? But true. Thanks to the both of them, I was a bit of a talented smarty pants kid back in the 80's. The teachers were amazed by what I knew because I was so young...

But this we will revisit; it becomes a little dramatic later on into the story.

Things started to take a turn for the worse once Aria turned two. I heard so many strange and scary noises, mostly in the evening hours. Some, I thought I could make out but others, I couldn't. Some were muffled noises; others were loud screams and uncontrollable crying. Every time I heard those noises, I was terrified.

On one of the many nights when I would wait for silence before approaching the door, I heard my mom sobbing. I approached my bedroom door and tried to peek to see what was going on, but I was yelled at immediately by the ogre, and the door slammed shut in my face.

I would lay in bed and just wait for the stillness of the night because it meant it was safe to approach the door. I went and opened the door slowly; at times it made this very screeching sound, so I had to be careful and open it cautiously. I didn't want to wake up the wrong person. I would find my mom on the floor in the corner of the room sitting with her knees to her chest as she held on to them rocking back and forth, quietly crying.

On this one night, was semi dark in the room, but I could clearly see that my mother was hurt, she had red marks all over her legs. As soon as she saw me, she tried pulling down her gown so I wouldn't see the marks, but I saw them.

She signaled for me not to make a noise as she pulled me in to hug me. As she hugged me, I heard her say over and over again, "I am sorry, I am so sorry." All I could say was, "I love you Mom."

When it was time to head back to bed, she walked me into my room, checked on my sister, and tucked us in like usual.

The next morning it was as if nothing had ever happened. My mom was in the kitchen with sweatpants on, so we wouldn't see the marks on her leg. The day went on as a bright, sunny day in a normal household, but I knew it was only a matter of time before it all got dark and chaos would storm through the door again.

One night, they argued over spilled milk that Mom forgot to clean up. I was peeking through the bedroom door and my mom waved at me to close the door. I didn't close it fast enough, so she shut it closed with her own body as I heard sounds of a belt hitting skin and of her crying and pleading for him to stop hitting her. The door shook so violently, I couldn't tell if I was shaking with it or *because* of it.

I tried my best not to make a sound. I didn't know what to do at that moment, but what I did know was that this man was physically hurting my mother, and I could be next.

I felt helpless, what could I do when I was only six years old?

I did all I could do to keep quiet. I placed both hands over my mouth as tears flowed down my face. I was terrified of becoming his next victim.

Chapter 5: Routines

My mom's daily routines included waking up at 4am to make ogre's breakfast and lunch. She helped with getting his clothes on. She would start with his pants, then the belt, and shirt as he sat down on a bench and waited for her to put on his socks and boots for work. I was surprised he was capable of putting on his own underwear.

Yes. Every single day my mother had to do this for a man who beat and hurt her endlessly. God forbid, she missed one of those steps, it was five across the face—her punishment. Depending on how severe the mistake she made, the punishment would be more intense.

Every morning, I'd listen in so that when he left, I could get up from my bed, open the door slowly to make sure the coast was clear, and exit the room with Aria. Most of the time I just wanted to make sure my mom wasn't hurt, the other times I just wanted to try to be a normal kid; I wanted to eat cereal, watch TV, and play with toys.

As I'd leave the room, I'd immediately see my mom cautiously glancing out the window to make sure he was gone. I'll never forget that facial expression of hers—relief. The way she would let out a huge breath as the ogre departed for work was gratifying to see, because I knew we had a few hours of normalcy.

She would then look at me and smile; mom grabbed both my hands as we twirled around in the living room. She would pick up my younger sister as we dropped to the floor in laughter as she tickled us.

Then once the fun was over, she'd proceed to cleaning the apartment thoroughly, as Aria and I played on the living room floor with our dolls.

Mom would start with making sure everything was where it belonged. Nothing could be out of place. She made sure dishes were done and the dinner making had begun. The only things that could be on the kitchen counter were the toaster and coffee maker. We had to make sure all of our toys were put away before he arrived.

Then, she would make sure that thirty minutes before his arrival, we were bathed, dressed and toys were put away in our toy box. Dinner had to be done, his clothes chosen for the evening, placed on the bed, and ready for when he arrived. We had to stand almost as if in a line up for inspection. He would then come in; she had to greet him with a big smile on her face and give him a kiss.

There was one time that I remember that Mom's kiss was not convincing. The ogre got so upset, that he grabbed her by her chin as he squeezed her lips together and started interrogating her in a very violent manner to find out what was wrong. In the meantime, my sister and I had to stand there in terror while this was happening.

Aria was so terrified she started to cry and she urinated herself. I noticed a rag on the counter, grabbed it, and tossed it on the floor where the urine was. I tried to dry it all while the ogre was busy correcting Mom.

Unfortunately, he realized what had happened, and as we saw him taking off his belt, both my sister and I started crying, screaming for him not to hit us. There was nothing my mother could do. As she stood there, she cried and pleaded with him to please stop hurting us with the belt; the ogre would not budge, and he continued with the beating. The times she did try to help us, she ended up getting hurt worse than us.

Eventually, once everything was over, we had to stay on the floor and wait till mom could approach us so she could get us cleaned up. Why? Because she still did not complete her duties with her husband. Because if she even thought of taking care of us first, the beating she would get would be even worse than what he already gave.

Mom had to help him get showered, help him dress and serve his dinner. The whole time Aria and I sat there in the puddle of urine, until he allowed my mom to get us cleaned up.

Mom comforted us while she showered us as we cried and cried. Once she finished getting us washed up, she fed us and got us into bed early. We cried ourselves to sleep that night, and like many nights like that one, bedtime was probably the only time we felt a remnant of safety knowing he could not hurt us while asleep.

The days turned into weeks, weeks turned into months, then Mom had a big bump where her stomach was; she was pregnant. Then, my sister Resne was born. I do not remember my mom ever having a baby shower for any of my sisters born in Springfield. I cannot recall my mom showing signs of happiness about being pregnant at all during those times. Not that she was not happy about us, but I think she could not enjoy any of her pregnancies because of him. Mom expecting another child did not delay or stop the abuse, not even for a moment.

One of the many rules Mom had to follow was that she was not allowed to leave the apartment without telling the ogre, and even then, only if he approved of it. The people living in the apartment building never really saw Mom while she was pregnant.

Most outings consisted of an escort, typically the ogre. He was the "big man" of the house, the money maker, therefore he decided what could be bought and what could be done. All receipts had to be submitted to him, and every penny accounted for or else she would face harsh consequences.

I remember when my mom visited her sister in Springfield, she was the only family she had there. Her other siblings and my grandmother lived in Puerto Rico. When Mom visited my aunt, it was only for a few hours. Not only because of the ogre but my mom was wary of my aunt's kids. Mom never wanted us to be alone with them. Mom always had to make sure we got back to the apartment on time, as if she had a curfew. When the hour to leave approached, she would start fidgeting and I would notice that it was time to go.

Upon our arrival to the apartment, it was all hands-on deck. My sister Aria and I helped mom as much as we could with her chores before the ogre got home.

The cleaning was the normal kind at first, you know the sweeping, wiping down counters, etc. Then it became more intense, scrubbing the floors on her knees with a brush, wiping down walls, among other detailed scrubbing. This was all because he wanted it that way. If he arrived from work and something was out of place and not done, my mom had to pay with the belt or his fists.

One afternoon, he arrived home from work and started yelling at mom because my Aria and I were playing in the living room and had some toys on the floor. Mom was good at keeping track of time. However, this time around she must have overlooked the living room to notice that we forgot to put our toys away. He immediately started yelling at her. He grabbed her by her hair, pulled her towards the living room, and threw her to the floor. There was a bucket with some water and a brush, he yelled at her to grab it, he kept pulling her hair, my mom's head bobbing everywhere as he pulled.

He screamed at her to scrub the floor, that if we wanted to play with toys, we had to pick them up. While all this was going on, my sister and I were in a corner of the apartment crying with fear. Suddenly, he rushed towards us, grabbed me by the arm so I could be standing while he hit me. In the blink of an eye the leather hit my skin with such force, it felt like burning fire slicing down my little legs. Mom watched helplessly as she sat on the floor next to the bucket that she was about to use to scrub. I was struck with the belt twice with such force he made me bleed, as soon as he was done, I ran into the room first, and Aria right after me.

She was three years old at the time, I'm not even sure if she could remember all of this, I pray she doesn't. I was almost seven years old, unfortunately for me, I remember.

After that incident, I discovered my imagination. As children we all have some type of creativity, right? Make believe, fantasy, whatever you want to call it. Well, mine was to invent a world for me to escape to. Somewhere to get away from the daily abuse I endured from the ogre.

I wanted to close my eyes and just imagine a world of happiness, a world of love, somewhere I could feel safe. I wanted to get away from it all. This world became my safe place from all the wickedness I was experiencing.

I used to fantasize and envision a world free from abuse and filled with love during those abusive periods.

In the real world, I wanted to believe that I was adopted; I thought there was no way this kind of life was for us. How can someone hurt us and not care? Was it because I was not his daughter? Is that why I got hit with the belt the most?

I could not help it; I imagined my real parents were in a faraway kingdom and that I was just their baby girl, that I was taken from them, and they missed me dearly.

Many times, I laid on my bed crying. If not, I just hunkered down by the corner of the bedroom until the coast was clear or until I fell asleep.

From then on, this imaginary world that I visited as often as I could, especially in those moments when I was beaten so badly, became the light I needed to get through the darkness.

Chapter 6: Creation of My Fairy World

It started as a dream one night after I cried myself to sleep. In the world of fairies, my name was "Aliandra," the long-lost daughter of King Theolis and Queen Isaidra in the kingdom of "Arstenia."

The story I created, that I was sent to the human world to live as a human, with the help of dark magic. I was taken by the evil ogre King, Aftare. He was an evil being who hated what the Kingdom of fairies stood for; righteousness, wisdom and most importantly, love. Each fairy was born with powers that would determine who they would become in their lives.

It was said that one day a fairy of noble blood would be born that would unite all kingdoms, fairy and ogres alike. So powerful that not even the dark magic would be able to destroy the powerful fairy. The ogre king suspected that the Princess "Aliandra" would be that special fairy. He couldn't destroy her, so he decided to send her away, with only himself and the nana, knowing her whereabouts.

That was my escape, my home away from the terror. I imagined myself being found by my loving fairy parents and living among them to fulfill my destiny.

Many times, I did wish it were all true, that I could just stay there and not come back to reality. The thought of my physical existence in the real world terrified me. Being a child with those feelings was not normal, but I had to deal with it however I could.

I was fearful of opening my eyes, of being awake, of hearing and seeing my mom cry every time the ogre left after hitting her or after throwing things all over the place.

I knew my make-believe fairy world was not real, but it was in moments like those, during the constant intimidation, that I felt comfort in knowing that one day I could have a reason to be happy again.

One afternoon, after being continuously struck with the belt for dropping some food on the floor, I ran to my room and crawled into bed. As I slowly covered myself with my blanket, I stared at the markings on my legs. I was in so much pain that I wept until exhaustion took over. I slowly opened my eyes and looked around and realized I was not in my room anymore. What was this place? I wondered. There were so many bright colors around me, so many birds chirping, the sounds of a soft calm wind. As I gazed ahead, I noticed a path with lots of beautiful flowers on both sides.

I started to walk and realized I was barefoot, walking on a dirt trail, but somehow my feet were clean. It didn't feel rough, the ground felt soft and smooth. There were a lot of butterflies around.

As I stood there some started to fly around me, so I extended my arms out to the side, and they gently landed on me. I started to giggle as I admired their colors.

I decided to start spinning around and around, they all slowly flew off as I ended up gently falling to the ground. While I lay there resting, I could hear someone singing, it was faint and soft but a very distinct sound. I sat up and started looking around to find where this beautiful voice was coming from. Next thing I know right in front of my eyes, a tiny person with wings flying was around me. I could not believe what I was seeing; I was in the presence of a fairy.

Excitement overtook my emotions. I jumped up from the ground and tried to catch it. I was stunned when I heard the fairy speak after I failed to catch her. At first it was hard to tell what the fairy was saying, but slowly and surely, I started to hear and understand her more clearly. She said her name was Kyra. The colors on her dress were blue, with a hint of purple and they blended so well together in the sunlight.

As she flew towards my bruised arm, I tried to cover it so she wouldn't see it. She then stopped midflight in front of me and touched my head with her wand; in doing so she made my bruises vanish. What just happened? Am I dreaming? I didn't want to know, I never wanted to leave this place. Kyra asked me if I was the long-lost princess; I was confused. I just shrugged my shoulders and told her I did not know.

Then out of nowhere, fairies started darting out from the flowers that were around me, all with a different color glow around them. They were all giggling and asking who I was. I bowed and introduced myself to the fairies.

All of them started flying down the path. I decided to follow, so I started to skip down the trail, and some followed behind, flying around me.

We headed down to the end of the lake; the water was crystal clear, and I could see right through it. There were a lot of fish in the water, all different colors and sizes. Kyra told me I can look into the water, and I'd be able to breathe in it. So, I did, and I could not believe my eyes; I was looking at mermaids, it was such an astonishing site.

They all had blonde hair and blue eyes. Their scales had shimmering rainbow colors, and they wore tube tops instead of a shirt. The bottom of the lake was white, instead of rocks, there were pillows; instead of Algi there were funny looking flowers under the water.

One of the mermaids swam up to me and introduced herself. Even under the water I could hear them so clearly. Her name was Maralia; she invited me to go into the water with her. I insisted I couldn't because I did not want to get wet and get in trouble. She then grabbed my hand and placed it in the water to show me that I could not get wet. My hand stayed dry! So, I sat on the edge of the lake and slowly got in the water.

Maralia held my hand as I started to swim with her to the bottom of the lake. At first, I was panicking holding my breath, and I got scared, but she insisted I did not have to do that. Maralia insisted for me to trust her and take a deep breath. I did as she asked, and I couldn't believe that I was breathing underwater.

As I finally made it to the bottom of the lake, I realized I was walking on a large bed of feathers; it was so soft and pretty. I sat on the rocks made from pillows while I watched the mermaids play hide and seek. The pillow rocks felt like silk, they felt comfortable and safe.

I watched everything happening above and around me. I was surrounded by so much joy and so much softness. It made me wonder, why was this happening to me? Was I permanently stuck here or was I going back home? Suddenly we all heard this loud growling sound, it turned out to be my stomach; I was very hungry. Maralia proceeded to take me back to the surface so I could find some food. Kyra and some of the other fairies were waiting for me to take me to their village. As I walked away from the lake and headed down the flower path, I looked up to trees as tall as buildings, and there was a big ball of light up ahead at the top of a hill.

As we got close to the village, the light wasn't as bright and I was able to see that up the hill there was a castle, with lots of different size roofs that looked like mushroom heads. At the top of that castle there was a mirror-like object that was the source of the brightness.

I felt out of place because I was bigger than the fairies, so Kyra found a solution. She gave me this small flower petal shaped like the sun. When I ate it, I became as small as Kyra and the others.

She told me not to worry about the light, it wasn't going to hurt me, they used it to scare ogres away. We proceeded to head over to this group of fairies that were dancing and eating. My stomach started to growl again; the sound was so loud the fairies around me got startled. Kyra knew what the sound was, she just giggled and told me to follow her.

Once we reached the table full of food, I sat down and took a moment to take in what I was seeing; there were so many different bright colors of food. Some I did not even know what they were, however, I was so hungry I did not care.

We all sat down around the table and Kyra gave thanks to mother earth for the food and enjoyed the food together.

Once the meal was done, I was taken up a hill by Kyra, at the end of that trail was that immense house with the bright mirror-like object on top that I had seen from afar. The mirror had a diamond-like surface, and the house did turn out to be a castle, but a small one.

There were fairy soldiers outside of this castle; they had smaller wings and were riding mice for horses. Instead of swords they had long funny shaped sticks. Their hats were made of branches and very small crystals. The soldiers immediately placed their weapons in front of the castle door, to stop us from entering.

They asked Kyra to introduce me and tell them the reason for our presence.

She explained to them how she needed to speak to the King and Queen, and how urgent it was. I was confused, I did not know what was so urgent. I could not understand what was going on. Once they allowed us to enter the castle, I could not help but stop and stare at everything around me. There were big trees all around me, I couldn't stop staring in awe.

Every single one of them had a different symbol on them. Kyra told me they represented the elements, fire, water, wind, and earth. At the very top of those trees was a dome-shaped window that had the bright light from the mirror shining right through and on to the floor. I ran to the middle of that light shining, held my arms out to the side and started spinning around until I felt dizzy. Everything here felt so full of life and joy that I couldn't help but feel it too.

As I sat down on the floor waiting for the room to stop spinning, I noticed Kyra down the other side of the room talking to two fairies, they were taller than the others for some reason.

The two fairies, (a man and a woman) had these sheer shinny gowns with strands of gold around them, and their wings were a lot longer and thinner. Their skin was as fair as mine, the woman had red hair with sky blue eyes and the man had dark black hair with emerald, green eyes. I don't think I had ever seen such beautiful beings.

They suddenly started to stare at me and eventually walked towards me. Not knowing what to do with myself, I slowly stood up to meet them. I realized then I was in the presence of the King and Queen of this fairyland.

They both kneeled in front of me, asked my name and wanted to know if I had a skin marking right below my neck. I pulled down my gown collar and showed them my birthmark.

They both looked at each other and held each other's hands, then took my hands and called me Aliandra.

They introduced themselves as King Theolis and Queen Isaidra and explained to me that I was their long-lost daughter taken away by an ogre king named Aftare. Both the king and queen could not help but just stare at me and smile so big. They pulled me into their arms and hugged me so tightly.

I felt so safe with so much warmth surrounding me, it was almost perfect.

I was confused, but happy at the same time. I wondered if this could be true, or if I was just dreaming. I hugged them, and they cried. They seemed to be so happy. They wanted to make an announcement to the fairy kingdom that their daughter had been found.

As we all started to walk towards the front entrance, there was a bright light and sounds of drums. The loud banging of the drums kept getting louder and louder the closer I got to the entrance.

One last loud sound went off along with happy cheers… then I opened my eyes. It was a dream. It felt so real. As I looked around, I realized I woke up back in my room and Aria was asleep next to me. Then a loud banging noise at the door made us get up from the bed; startled, I walked towards the door while my sister started to cry as she covered her ears. I then opened the door just enough to look and there I saw the ogre yelling at my mother.

She was just standing there covering her face with both hands while tears flowed down her cheeks.

I slowly and very quietly closed the door and headed back to bed to lay next to Aria. She was still very scared, so much so she was shaking. I covered her ears so she wouldn't hear the yelling as much, all while trying to calm her down. We both just laid there until the noises in the other room stopped and nothing but silence was all around us.

I remember one time my mother was taking a shower, and Aria and I were right outside the door trying to get her to open the door. It got to the point where we cried for her, because we did not want to be alone with him in the living room.

He got annoyed and very angry by our crying to Mom; he got up to get a belt, and while we were at the door, he beat us, over and over again—so badly the belt cut my skin, and I saw blood.

My mother heard us; she opened the bathroom door so we could go in there while he was still yelling at us. She tried to comfort us as best she could. She checked our skin where we were hit and hugged us. We sat there, crying together, and Mom apologized over and over again.

The ogre yelled from outside the bathroom door to hurry up and get out. Infuriated still, as soon as my mom came out of the bathroom he grabbed her by the wet hair, yelled, and started to swing the belt on her. Her skin was still wet, ensuring it would hurt even more.

In the meantime, my sister and I yelled and cried, "No! Please stop, leave her alone!" but it just made him even more angry. He shoved us so hard we fell on the floor. We crawled to the corner of the wall, where my mom ran up to us, covered us with her body so we would not get hit with the belt again. Still bare skin she continued to get assaulted by the ogre, with no mercy in sight he continued to hit her. Without even a piece of clothing to shield her from the relentless swing of the belt, she endured agonizing pain to protect us. He then lowered himself down by mom's side while grabbing her face with one hand and said to her, "If you interfere again, it will be even worse for them."

Once he was satisfied with the damage he'd done, he yelled at my mom to get dressed and clean the kitchen. When we tried to flee to the safety of our room, he stopped us and yelled for us to stay in the corner until he said so. Aria and I just cried and hugged each other while fear overcame us. We sat in a state of shock, terrified.

After Mom finished cleaning the kitchen, she took his beer to the living room where he was seated, watching his tv shows. With a quiver in her voice, she asked him if she could remove us from the corner. He angrily turned away from the TV and with this face full of viciousness, nodded "yes" while slamming his beer on the table.

Mom helped us up from the corner in which we were helplessly sobbing and took us to the bedroom. She got us ready for bed and after taking a beating like that, we made sure we slept. My baby sister Resne slept safe and sound, thankfully, away from the chaos.

As soon as I calmed down and closed my eyes, I went to the kingdom of "Arstenia" where my lovely and true parents awaited my return. That is where I wanted to be; that is where I always thought I belonged.

The kingdom of Arstenia was amazing for little me. The color of the trees was like no other; trees shimmering in different colors as the wind blew them so blissfully. The rivers crystal clear; they were so clear that I could see all the bright colored gems that looked like corrals at the bottom. As I treaded water in the river, the fishes swam all around me. I started reaching for the bottom, where the pillow-like floor awaited me.

Once submerged I saw my mermaid friends; they held my hand, and I could suddenly breathe underwater again. They then proceeded to take me to explore their heavenly underwater world until they took me back to the surface, where my fairy friends were waiting. My nightgown was instantly dried by their magic, which made me laugh uncontrollably because it tickled me so terribly.

Shrunken by them to their size, we played in the Fairy Field. It was full of flowers, the most beautiful ones I have ever seen, my favorite ones were the bell-shaped ones. We played until it was time to eat. We ate with their families, I got to know everyone, and enjoyed every moment, fear free.

Once I finished my day playing by the lake and the Fairy Field, I headed to the castle where my parents awaited my return. King Theolis and Queen Isaidra were very gentle and kind to me. Everything was so full of love and joy in my paradise. Queen Isaidra had some resemblance to Mom, and she was so happy. I always wondered if I would ever see Mom this joyful too.

But with all things in life coming to an end, as I grew older my imaginary world came to me less and less. My safe haven was slowly but surely starting to fade away.

Chapter 7: My Farewell To The Fairy World

By the time I reached the age of nine years old, I noticed I was not able to connect with my fairy world as easily. Any time I would fall asleep or try to daydream about them, it became clear I was losing my connection to my safe haven. Any time I reached the forest the colors were not as bright and vibrant as before; at least the fairies still welcomed me with open arms each time.

The lake was as beautiful as always; however, I noticed it was getting harder and harder to breathe underwater; because of this I could not play as much with my mermaid friends. Once I headed down to the castle to see the King and Queen, I got excited to see them again because they treated me as their own and I always felt welcomed.

The castle guards always saluted me with kindness and respect. They announced my arrival as the doors opened. When I saw the king and queen waiting for me at the entrance, I ran up to them and gave them a big hug.

Hugging them, I noticed our height difference, how tall I had gotten. My head reached the height of their chest area. When I first arrived, I had only been able to reach the height of their hip.

The king noticed it as well; he looked over at the queen and told her how much I had grown up.

Heading over to the garden area together, the king explained to me that due to my growth I was going to lose access to this world, and how that was a good thing because I was becoming a young lady. I instantly started crying and held onto him tight.

I expressed how growing up was not something I wanted to do. I desired to stay there with them and not go back to that apartment. The queen kneeled in front of me, grabbed both my hands, kissed them and told me everything was going to be just fine. She insisted it was the way the curse worked; I was never supposed to remain in their world.

It comforted the queen to know she was able to play a part in showing me that even though we can't always get what we want, we can be assured there is a better ending to our stories that will make us great again.

On the other hand, they were happy to meet me and spend so much time with me, and we made amazing memories in the process.

It was time for them to let me go with sadness in their hearts, and I witnessed the moment when they realized that although I would succeed on my own, they would never see me again.

It humbled them in knowing I was going to become a force to be reckoned with; this persuaded them to accept my next chapter in life in becoming a successfully mature young lady. It was such a hard thing to accept myself, but I had no choice.

That night, we said goodbye, and we never crossed paths in my dreams again.

Chapter 8: Imperfections

A year went by, and the abuse continued. There was never any reprieve during those years. By that point, my mother had my sister Mirla when I was about to be nine years old.

Some mornings when I'd wake up before my sisters, I would sit on the bed, pull the blankets off me, lift my sleeping gown and examine my skin. I would start by counting the scratches and bruises I had. I even started comparing their sizes and colors. I knew that the purple bruises were the new ones, while the ones turning yellowish were the old ones.

Fresh scratches were a reddish color, while the older ones scabbed over. I would wander deep into thought and just replay what moments and events caused all of my injuries. Images replayed in my head of the horrible occurrences that had happened. Uncontrolled tears would just slide down my cheeks as I thought to myself, "Will this ever end?"

I felt like a target. I always had a feeling of not belonging and not being wanted. The ogre made it known he felt hatred towards me. The words, "you are not my daughter" were frequently yelled by him. If my mom stepped out of the room, the only thing I could feel was terror. I knew what he was capable of, I feared what he would do. I often followed my mom around the house due to that reason. The farther away I could get from him, the less scared I was.

Attending school was great for me because it meant I got away from it all for a few hours. But for the ogre, it meant something else.

Going to school every day was the best part of my days. I could be away and not worry, even if just for a few hours, it didn't matter because I felt free. Every morning, Mom made sure she dressed us accordingly; she had to make sure that any bruises that were visible, were covered. I remembered always wearing long pants and long sleeve blouses to cover any bruises. I do not recall ever wearing a T-shirt to school, or even a dress.

Many times, I left to go to school and felt like I was dressed like a boy.

We also got the daily speech of not saying a word to anyone of what had happened at home, especially when we went to school. We were told how we would be taken away and we would never see our mom again if we told anyone. What child wanted to hear something like that? It was cruel to hear, and we heard it a lot, but we believed it. Every time.

It became harder to hide any physical injuries from people I encountered. I remember getting sick at school once. The teacher immediately sent me to see the nurse. I was petrified. I thought to myself, *this is it, she is going to see my bruises, and I am going to be in so much trouble. I was going to be taken away and never see my mother or my sisters again.*

The hallway to the nurse's office looked further and further with every step I took. My stomach started hurting more than before, I even felt weak. I ended up holding on to the wall as I walked. The voices of my mom and the ogre suddenly rushed through my thoughts repeatedly: "Don't tell anyone about anything that happens at home," "hide your bruises," keep your sleeves down and your shirt tucked in," "you don't want them to take you away from us do you?"

As the pain intensified, I couldn't help but start to cry as I held my stomach. I was halfway to the nurse's office when a teacher saw me. He held my hand as we both finished walking to my destination—the room that was going to be my end.

I had to think quickly about what I was going to tell the nurse if she discovered any of the markings on my skin.

I entered the room, and there she was with a concerned facial expression as she saw the agony I was in. They helped me lay down on a small couch. The teacher left telling me I was in good hands. I was still crying, holding onto my stomach. The nurse asked me questions about what I was feeling, and she tried to calm me down. I began panicking as she rubbed my stomach, fearing she'd lift my shirt and notice my bruises.

As she felt around my stomach, I held my breath in hopes that she wouldn't notice just how much pain I was in. I wanted to scream. She noticed that I flinched as she touched my belly. As she tried to lift my shirt, I pulled it down at the same time. The nurse said, "Sweetheart, I just want to look at your tummy." I frantically shook my head, no, as I cried louder, so loud that I screamed. She got startled and told me she would call my mom so she could pick me up and take me home. I instantly agreed.

Once my mom arrived, I was relieved. I wondered how she got to the school so fast since she did not drive or own a car. Of course, as I set foot outside and looked into the distance, there was the ogre waiting in the vehicle for us. My heart plummeted. The first five minutes of the drive home were silent. I could see him looking at me every now and then through the rear-view mirror. He then asked me, "Did anyone see your bruises?" I shook my head as I still held my stomach in pain. My mother tried to tell him that I had to see a doctor. He told her to shut up instead. Mom just stared out the window till we arrived at the apartment.

I went straight to my bed to lay down. Mom came into the room with some warm rags to place on my stomach. She lifted my shirt and covered her mouth in shock and fear as she saw the bruises on my ribs. I could see the tears falling down her cheeks. I reached up to wipe them from her face and she hugged me, whispering how sorry she was.

Chapter 9: The Closet

One morning as I stretched in bed, I noticed something different. As I slowly opened my eyes there was a glimmer of a light shining on my face. It was the bedroom door slightly open, and the living room light was shining in. I could hear the ogre screaming at Mom. I looked to my left and noticed something that made me shiver with fear and panic started to rise.

Oh no! It was the closet! The closet that was not supposed to be open when my sisters and I were in the room…it was half-opened. It was the ogre's private closet. He used the closet in our bedroom, I did not know what for at the time, all I knew was that we were not to ever, *ever* open it. I got up as quietly as possible and I closed the closet door very slowly and very carefully.

I could still hear him yelling, so I quietly went over to my bedroom door, and peeked. Though I heard the yelling, I could not see him or my mom. Then I saw him pacing from the kitchen to the living room. I could hear my mom crying now. I stepped a little further out and could see her standing as still as she could, the terror in her face telling me what was coming.

He then proceeded to scream in her face and even spat at her. I knew what would follow, so I tried to avoid it by walking quietly back into bed and pretending I was still asleep. Next thing I knew he threw the door open. He started pulling me by my legs and screaming, "Where is it? What did you do with it? Why were you looking in the closet? You are not allowed in there!"

All I could do was cry unconsolably, barely able to respond. The few words I was able to get out in a shaky voice were: "I didn't do it," "No! Don't hit me," "Mommy please help me!"

The whole time he was yelling, my mom was digging through that closet like our lives depended on it. I mean clothes, hangers and toys were all over the bedroom floor. She finally found what he was looking for. All I remember was seeing some small bags with white stuff in them. He immediately grabbed them, violently pushing my mom down to the floor to get her out of the way.

At that point my other sisters were awake and crying as well. My mom got on the bed with us and held us tight while we all sobbed and tried to recover from the terror we were left with. She kept saying to us "I'm here, it's ok. I am here. I'm sorry. I'm so sorry."

As he left the apartment, he slammed the front door as he headed down the stairs, we could hear him yelling, "What are you looking at? Mind your own business!" Our neighbors heard the screams, they were waiting outside their apartments, being inquisitive as usual, but not trying to do anything to help. Fuming with rage, he dashed down the stairs. Every floor he went to, he made it clear to everyone observing that he was a dangerous man.

We did not see him for the rest of the day. In the meantime, we helped Mom put everything neatly back in the closet.

She had us promise we would never, *ever* try to open that closet, no matter how curious we were. I promised her that I did not open it, and that I was not sure how it had happened.

My sister Aria, who was closest to me in age, started crying and admitted it was her. She told her, "It was me mommy, I was looking for my dolly, sorry." My mom hugged her even tighter and told her, "It's ok, just don't do it again, next time get me. Ok? Just get me first."

Fortunately, the ogre appeared later that night as if nothing had occurred and we all continued to behave as though nothing had happened.

Chapter 10: The Reality Of It All

Weeks went by without incident. Truthfully though, there were some wonderful days like those without incident that felt dream-like. For a while, we felt secure. He took us shopping for new clothes, toys, and even took us to the park. I could not help but wonder, could this be it? Is it done? Could we finally be a normal family?

No. There was no such thing as that for us.

A person's life can be left severely harmed by all that chaos. I personally cannot remember much happiness; it was not something I recall experiencing as much growing up in that household. When trying to remember, only one fun memory came to mind. When winter came around, we had snow days that made us jump with joy.

The snowball fights at the bus stop were the best. I had a friend there, her name started with the letter "V" and, she always protected me from the other kids. She was older than me and a lot taller. She always treated me as if I was her little sister, no one dared to bother me with her by my side.

I remember asking my friend "V" if I could go live with her. I told her that I did not want to go home, and I think she suspected something was going on. I am sure everyone did in that building and the surrounding homes but in those days no one wanted to get involved, no one wanted to interfere. People were either scared, or they just did not care enough to do anything about it.

Trying to recollect the good memories seems like trying to reach for something that is not there. Everything is so clouded with the memory of my trauma that it feels like there are things missing. Snapshots of moments and people aren't enough for me but then again, were there any happy times worth remembering other than a friend that made me feel safe and a memory of the most wonderful time of the year actually being wonder-filled?

During Christmas break, my neighborhood friends and I always made sure to enjoy ourselves in the snow. I always felt like the ogre had a secret motive, because that was the one occasion he insisted on me going outside. We spent so much time outside playing that, looking back, I'm shocked we didn't get frostbite.

The days leading up to Christmas day were something every child looked forward to. However, I can say I honestly do not have any holiday memories during those years in Springfield. I cannot even picture a Christmas tree, stockings, not even presents.

I think that part of my brain perhaps could not hold on to any good moments I might have had of Christmas. It seemed the bad memories overtook the good memories if there were any. It's as if it never really made a healthy enough impression on my memories for my brain to retain it.

Chapter 11: Running Away

My mom tried to get away so many times. However, of all of them, only three of those times were enough to lodge themselves into my memories, the last attempt being the most impactful.

The first time my mom was ready to run, I can't even remember why the ogre hit her. It was the afternoon after my mom received another physical encounter, she waited for the ogre to go in the shower, and she quietly grabbed us and ran across the street. I remember it being some type of financial institution, like a bank.

I remember seeing staff standing behind a glass, and people forming lines. Across, there were a few desks with people working on computers. My mom ran in there with us, but the security guard immediately stopped us. My mom did not speak English well, so I did the interpreting for her. My mom said, *"Dile que nos ayude por favor, que llamen la policia."* I told the security guard "Can someone please help us? Call the police for us! Please!"

As the seconds passed, my mom was becoming more frantic and anxious. She began to cry. The security guard just said, "Sorry ma'am, you can't be here. I am going to have to ask you to leave." I yelled at the officer, "No! You don't understand! He is going to find us, and he will hurt my mom." A man with a business suit came out, pulled the security guard to the side and spoke to him in a low voice. I couldn't hear what he said but once they were done speaking, the guard approached us and said, "Please ma'am, you must leave. We can't get involved. Please, I need my job. Please just go."

I struggled to understand what was happening while my mom pushed us towards the door to leave. Did they really not care? I asked her why they wouldn't help us. She just said, *"Todo va estar bien."* In English it meant, "Everything is going to be ok."

The whole time we were there, everyone just stared at us. Some of them looked embarrassed to us. Some of them looked scared...No one approached us to offer help.

As we crossed the street, we could hear the ogre's loud howl; it was frightening. He was calling out my mom's name, his voice sounded so thunderous. He had started running down the steps looking for us. Once we saw him, we all knew what would happen next. The consequence had to fit the crime, and we all paid the price—Mom of course got it the worst.

My sister Aria and I got a butt whooping. Afterwards, we were shoved into our rooms and left to watch the two youngest ones. We did not even dare open the door to see what was going on. We heard a lot of commotion; we heard items being thrown and smashed on the floor and we listened as they broke upon impact. I pulled my sisters away from the door and got them on the beds so we could sleep or at least try to. I made sure they were tucked in, and that night, almost routinely, we cried ourselves to sleep.

The next morning, we stepped outside of our room with caution and as we looked around. We saw all the damage left from the mayhem that had occurred the previous night, after our failed attempt to escape.

The ogre, thankfully, was nowhere to be seen, so we immediately started looking for our mom. We found her on the kitchen floor picking up pieces of debris, her eyes so swollen from all the crying we could hardly see them. Her right eye was purple and closed shut; he had hit her pretty badly. It was a startling sight.

I noticed she had a cloth wrapped around her upper arm, with red big spots soaking through. He had injured her so severely that she was bleeding, but then, at the time, I didn't realize what it really was.

She saw us and told us not to get any closer because we were going to get our feet cut from the debris she was picking up. We stopped walking towards her and looked around. I then grabbed the broom, Aria got the dustpan, and we attempted to help our mom—we didn't do a very good job, but she appreciated it nonetheless. Once the floor was clear, she huddled us in and gave us a big hug. As we cushioned ourselves in her arms, she graciously and with such caution tried to fix our hair and clean our faces. She stayed looking at us for a few minutes, until she suddenly started tickling us until our stomachs hurt from all the laughter. For that moment, we had forgotten.

As we sat on the floor she looked at me and told me in Spanish, *"Voy a encontrar a alguien quien nos ayude,"* which means, "I will find someone to help us." She continued to say, *"Yo se que Dios no nos ha abandonado,"* meaning, "I know God has not abandoned us."

Before that moment, the mention of God was foreign to me. I wondered who this "God" was. Because we never went anywhere, I had no idea what a church was, let alone who God was.

Why is mom saying he won't abandon us? I was not sure what she meant but it gave mom hope, so I wanted to believe what she was saying too. From that day on, she taught us to talk to "God," someone that we could not see but apparently was always watching over us. It became necessary to ask him for help, so we did. Everyday.

Did it help? I think it did. It was enough to give us hope to keep pushing forward.

PART 2

Chapter 12: Ogre's wrath

One particular day, the apartment was extremely quiet as the ogre was not there. It was a weekend and we were home all day. I was not sure if I should have been excited or scared that he was not there with us, but the thought of him worried me.

Suddenly, we heard a knock at our apartment door. My mom looked through the window and she proceeded to open the door. My sisters and I immediately ran to the kitchen and stared at the intruder from the table. There was a man with a light brown Afro standing there talking to Mom. He spoke Spanish, and he also had a mustache, a funny looking one too. He saw us and told my mom, "Wow, they are all so big. Hi girls!" We all cautiously waved our hands at him. My sisters and I were curious and kept getting closer and closer to the door. We wanted to know what they were talking about. Who was this man?

He asked mom for the ogre. My mom told him he was not home and told him it was not a clever idea for him to be there or for her to even be talking to him. He chuckled and said, "It's fine, that's my buddy." As he was about to open his mouth to say something else the ogre appeared out of nowhere at the doorway, incredibly angry. The expression on his face was unforgettable; he looked like he was about to kill someone. His nostrils were flared, his gaze was intense, and his fists were clenched so tight that his knuckles turned white. He grabbed the man by his Afro, yanked him to the floor, beat him repeatedly all while screaming at him. The man's face was so bloody, we could not even see his eyes anymore.

All the commotion started grabbing the attention of the neighbors. They all looked outside their windows and doors to see what was happening. The ogre started dragging him down the apartment building steps, one by one, dragging him by the hairs on his head. The guy kept on yelling the whole way down, he tried to remove the ogre's clutches from his afro, but it did not work. Mom was petrified. She closed the door and started to breathe so heavily; panic started to set in. We all ran to the windows to see where we could get a better view. The ogre dragged the guy all the way to his vehicle.

There was one lady that lived above us—she was always so nice to my mom and, I liked her. As the ogre was causing a scene, she knocked at our door. Mom answered and we could see that the lady was concerned. She wanted to see how my mom was doing and asked her, "Do you need help?" The lady's husband showed up and pulled on her arm and said, "Come on, let's go, it's none of our business." My mom then grabbed her arm and with a terrified look in her eyes and a trembling voice said, *"Por favor no te vayas,"* meaning, "Please don't go."

At that exact moment, the ogre came back and started yelling at the lady. "What are you doing? Mind your own business!" He then directed his anger to the lady's husband and told him, "Keep your woman under control." She got so mad, she started yelling at the ogre "Women are meant to be loved, protected, and respected not mistreated and hurt. Unlike you, my husband respects me, protects me, and loves me," she yelled.

The ogre yells, "My woman respects me!" The lady yelled back. "No! She fears you, that is not respect or love!" The lady's husband pulled her by the arm one last time and took her up the steps. Her husband just kept on telling her, "Please babe, let's just go, please." Now that I think about it, the lady had more guts than her husband. She was not scared of the ogre.

The ogre was not happy at all. He finished taking out his anger on my mother. He shoved her back into the apartment, and she fell to the floor, sobbing, pleading with him, *"Por favor no me des,"* meaning, "Please don't hit me." At that point, we ran to the living room. I was trying so hard not to let him hear me cry, I covered my own mouth. Dishes were pushed over the counter and on the floor. He picked up a small knife, and with intense fury, he got my mom off the floor, slammed her hand on to the counter, and with the knife, he started cutting the top part of her hand.

Her long piercing scream was deafening, so loud I am sure it was heard all around the apartment building. He told her with anger and threat in his voice "I don't want any man here. Do you understand that?" She screamed, crying, *"No hice nada! Te lo prometo, no hice nada!"* meaning, "I didn't do anything! I promise, I did nothing!" She was desperate to get him off of her. Till this day it is unbearable to remember that moment, I can still hear her ear-piercing screams.

As he released her hand, she fell to the floor, and he did a complete 180. His whole facial expression changed from a monster full of rage to a worried human being. He went down on his knees beside her and told her *"Sabes te amo, entiende que me pongo tan celoso, no quiero perderte,"* translating to, "You know I love you, I get so jealous, I don't want to lose you."

He grabbed her and pulled her in for a hug. She kept crying because she was in so much pain. He ripped a piece of fabric from his T-shirt and wrapped it around my mother's hand and even kissed it like she would kiss one of our booboos. Just remembering this makes me sick to my stomach, it makes me feel like I am right there again.

He went ahead to help her pick up everything he knocked down to the floor, and when he got a chance, kissed her forehead, as if that were his apology. As if a kiss was going to make the bleeding stop. As if repeatedly saying "I'm sorry" and "I love you" would erase the damage he has caused.

I kept my sisters in the room; I did not want them to see any of what was going on.

The rest of the afternoon and evening went on like nothing ever happened. My mom finished taking care of her wound, she tucked us into bed, and off to sleep we went.

That night as I slumbered, I woke up in a forest. I was lying on a bed of flowers. As I sat up, there was a figure beside me, with the brightest light I have ever seen. I tried looking directly at the light, but it was too dazzling for my eyes. I looked away, placed my hands over my face and started to cry. I could hear this voice say, "Don't cry little one, you are not alone. I am with you."

I suddenly woke up and was back in my room. As I sat up on my bed, I pondered about what had just happened. Where did I go.? What did I see.?

All of a sudden, as I looked around the room, I realized my mom was there. She pointed her finger over her closed lips to *shhh*. I woke up my sisters as quietly as I could, and Mom quickly got us dressed. She had bags ready to go for us, seemingly, before she even woke us up.

As we quietly exited the apartment, I noticed how dark it was outside. We carefully and silently went down the steps of the apartment building, we crossed the street and caught a bus. When we got off the bus, we walked toward a row home. I did not recognize it, but it turned out it was my aunt's house at the time.

My mom knocked once, then twice. No answer. Every knock following those became louder and louder and more desperate, to the point where my mom started calling out her name. Still no answer. Noticing my mom's desperation, I started knocking and yelling out her name with her. Hearing our yelling, my younger sisters started crying. Once Mom realized her sister was not going to answer, she fell to her knees and broke down to cry. Worried about what would happen next, I started wailing as well. She didn't wait long before she gathered us and our things, and we started walking.

I can remember seeing a lot of big buildings all around us as we walked. Some looked like looming giants, as the skyscrapers pierced the sky like swords. I wondered if we could enter one of them and get help because we were so tired from walking. It was so late in the night, we just wanted to sleep. We told Mom we wanted to go home. She told us we couldn't, and we arrived at some steps that seemed to go on forever. The building at the top of the steps looked like a museum or a library, I'm still not sure what it was.

We sat there and Mom huddled us around her She embraced us to keep us warm. The wind was beating us from every side. After being there for a while, a police officer approached us. He said, "Ma'am you can't stay here. You're going to have to go elsewhere." My mom shook her head and said "Please." I told him we didn't have anywhere to go; we could not go back home.

He sharply replied, "I don't care where you go, you just can't stay here." I started crying, then my sisters followed. By a stroke of luck, or humanity, it seemed his heart had softened a little because as we got up to walk away, he said, "Look, if you go down the street from here there is a shelter. They might still be open but I'm not sure. Good luck."

We kept walking until we came to the shelter. We made it just in time before they closed the doors. Once in the building I looked around and saw so many people laid in these small beds. I remember they only had one small bed left, so we laid down as best we could and tried to sleep. I noticed my mom stayed awake. When I asked her why, she told me we could not trust anyone and we had to be careful.

I want to say we probably slept for about 2 hours or so before we were woken by my mom's sudden scream. Shaking I opened my eyes to see. I saw that there was a guy with his hands under the sheets touching my mom. We got up immediately. She pushed him away and we ran out of there.

After walking down a couple of blocks, my mom made the painful decision of returning to the apartment building. We waited for the bus back home and returned to the misery that slept just beyond the front door.

I want to say God was looking out for us that night. When we returned, the ogre had not even realized that we were gone; he was snoring so loudly, we could hear him outside the door.

One by one, we quietly went inside the apartment and straight to our room. After making sure we were in bed and quiet, my mom sneaked into her bed as if she had been there the entire time.

The next morning, we went back to the same order of things. We heard him head out to work on his work bus and got up right after to get ready for school. I was never sure what my mom did once he left that day. Maybe she took the time to plan our next great escape.

Chapter 13: Unfortunate Realities

In what would have possibly been the best years of my young life, I was instead stuck in the middle of a never-ending storm of chaos and hopelessness. This is because the ogre ruined any chance, I had of truly excelling. I was a very bright kid in the mid 80's and 90's. As I mentioned earlier, it was all thanks to my mom's only friend. Every time she visited when I was a toddler, she taught me colors, numbers, how to write my name, etc.

First grade, second grade, and third grade teachers had a hard time keeping me busy, because everything they taught me, I already knew, making it boring. My mom was called to school once, because the teacher, Mrs. Sargeant, wanted to show her my accomplishments. As it turns out, I also had a knack for art. I could draw pretty much anything.

My mom did not know because I only drew at school, since I didn't have any materials at home to draw. Mom and the ogre went to the school for the meeting. He thought the teacher was going to complain about me. They were both left speechless once the teacher started pulling out all the art that she had saved that I drew.

As Mrs. Sargeant told her how smart I was, and how I could benefit from taking a knowledge test so they could skip me to 8th grade, the ogre's expression changed. In fact, I became afraid of it. The teacher's words to my mother did not sit well with him.

My mom noticed his lack of interest as well. She told the teacher she did not want me to do any of that. I was so upset Mom had turned the teacher's offer down. Mrs. Sargeant then grabbed a piece of paper from her desk—it had some information written down—and she told them, "Here. Just in case you change your mind. Here is the information to the school with the name and phone number of the person you would meet. You have a very promising young lady here." Mom grabbed the paper, thanked her, and we all walked out of her classroom.

The car ride home was incredibly quiet. Once we got to the apartment, I could hear him talking to Mom about the meeting. He expressed to her how it was a bad idea, and he did not want me around those bigger kids. Yet, my mom had somehow convinced him to just take a tour of the school first. Later that month, we visited the middle school, and I remember enjoying it so much. When they informed my mother of everything they could do to increase my skill and knowledge, her approval was so obvious. She was overjoyed.

Naturally, the ogre was not at all thrilled. Once we left, he immediately told my mom how much he did not like the idea of me going to this school. "I forbid her to take any test. She is not going to any other school. I don't care how smart she is. It's not happening," he demanded. I cried. It was not fair; I was looking forward to being at this school. My mom did not speak a word once he said that. She just stared at nothing, into empty space, as he talked. I was very upset, but I knew I couldn't blame my mom. Her hands were tied.

Later that night, after we arrived home from the middle school, we had received some really upsetting news. It only made the hopeless day worse. Her only friend that used to come over to the apartment to teach me, was killed by her husband while she was expecting a child. I will never forget that moment, my mom's one and only friend gone because of another ogre. I could hear mom talking on the phone about how her friend's ogre used to abuse her. Just thinking about the gruesome manner of her death, even just remembering my mom talking about it was painful.

By some miracle, her baby somehow survived. Somehow in the midst of the chaos around us, there was a beacon of light in that dark gruesome moment. So, here was my question after finding out something like this, where was this man called God my mom talked to every night? Did Mom's friend ever ask Him for help? Why didn't God help Mom's friend? Why did He allow that to happen? What are my mom's chances of surviving her own ogre? The one thing I knew for sure was that I did not want to lose my mom. God and I were going to talk that night.

At bedtime, I got on my knees by my bedside and talked with God. I spoke to him about mom's friend and her baby. I asked why. I got no answer. I then asked him not to abandon my mom or my sisters like everyone else has. I asked him if Mom was ever meant to be happy—no answer.

After kneeling and begging God for answers for so long I lost track of time, I realized this was a one-way conversation and all I could do was hope that someone, somewhere, by some miracle, would show us some kindness, and maybe even save us.

I am not going to lie; I was upset at God. Why were we subjected to such pain if He loved us as Mom claimed? Did we not deserve a life filled with love and peace?

Did we not deserve a life with some normalcy? Was this His way of building us up for a better life later? I couldn't understand the point of any of it.

After that night, my mom made a decision...

We either tried to escape again for good or died attempting to do nothing at all. We had to find a way out of this nightmare we were living.

Chapter 14: A Glimmer Of Hope

Around this time, I was nine years old; my sister Aria was six years old; Resne was four years old, and Mirla was two years old.

It was Fall; the leaves had begun to change color and were littering the ground, and the air was cold as soon as you stepped outside. I remember it being a Saturday because we were watching all of our favorite cartoons. A knock on the door prompted the ogre to quickly get up and approach my mother. "Are you expecting someone?" Mom shook her head no.

He walked over to the door and lifted the small curtain over the door window. When he saw who it was, he hesitated to open the door. There was a very pretty older woman standing on the other side of the door, with black hair and skin like the warm color of cinnamon. It was my grandmother, my mother's mom. I didn't remember her; I was a toddler last time she saw me.

It was, however, her first time meeting my sisters. My mom saw who was at the door and ran to her. My mom and grandmother held each other while they cried. On the other hand, the fact that my grandmother had just arrived without an invitation made the ogre nervous. His behavior changed completely; I could tell he was taken by surprise.

She saw all four of us just sitting on the living room floor and got down on her knees to sit next to us. She hugged us, one by one and started playing with us, tickling us, and even braided our hair. She had a big mole right next to her nose, and I remember my baby sister Mirla flicking it. My grandma would laugh; her laughter was funny because she held it in and it sounded muffled. The house was filled with so much laughter while she played with us, it was such a rare sound. My grandmother only spoke Spanish, while I understood her, it was difficult for me to have a conversation with her seeing as how my Spanish was not good, and I rarely practiced it.

My mom offered her coffee, so my grandmother got up from the floor and walked over to the kitchen. While we continued to play in the living room, the adults talked in the kitchen. I even heard them laughing, it seemed so normal, yet...so out of sorts.

Little did I know, my grandmother had heard rumors about what was going on with my mom and her abusive partner, boyfriend, fiancée, whatever he was. My grandmother wanted to see for herself if there was any truth to the rumors.

When the ogre was not around, I heard my mother tell her at first, everything was ok, however my grandmother was not convinced. They were both siting at the dining room, when she grabbed her hands and held them in hers, kissed her hand and told her "You don't have to be afraid anymore, I am here to help," in Spanish, *"Ya no tengas mas miedo, estoy aqui para ayudar."* My mother started to quietly cry and leaned forward as my grandmother hugged her. She was still too afraid to speak. They finally got up and decided to call it a night and talk another day.

I, of course, quietly tippy toed to bed so they wouldn't see that I was ease dropping.

As I laid in bed that night, I just thought to myself, could this be it? Are we finally getting away? We were soon to find out.

Chapter 15: Aware And Ready

For the next few days while my grandmother stayed at the apartment, the ogre behaved. Little did he know, once he left to go to work, it was my grandmother's time to interrogate Mom about what was going on. I have no doubt that the ogre intimidated my mother into keeping quiet at some point.

The talks that my grandmother had with my mother for any confirmation of what was going on was futile. Mom was too terrified to say anything; she feared for our lives. Nonetheless, it did not matter that she did not answer grandma's questions. Within just a week of her being there, the ogre did not disappoint. It was too much time for him to spend without being abusive towards my mom.

My grandmother woke up in the middle of the night, because she heard some noises in the kitchen. She looked out of the room towards the kitchen, but no one was there. As she walked over to my mom's sleeping area, she turned on the light to a terrifying scene.

She saw the ogre standing next to mom's bedside. My mother was lying in bed sleeping, and he was standing next to her with a kitchen knife in his hand.

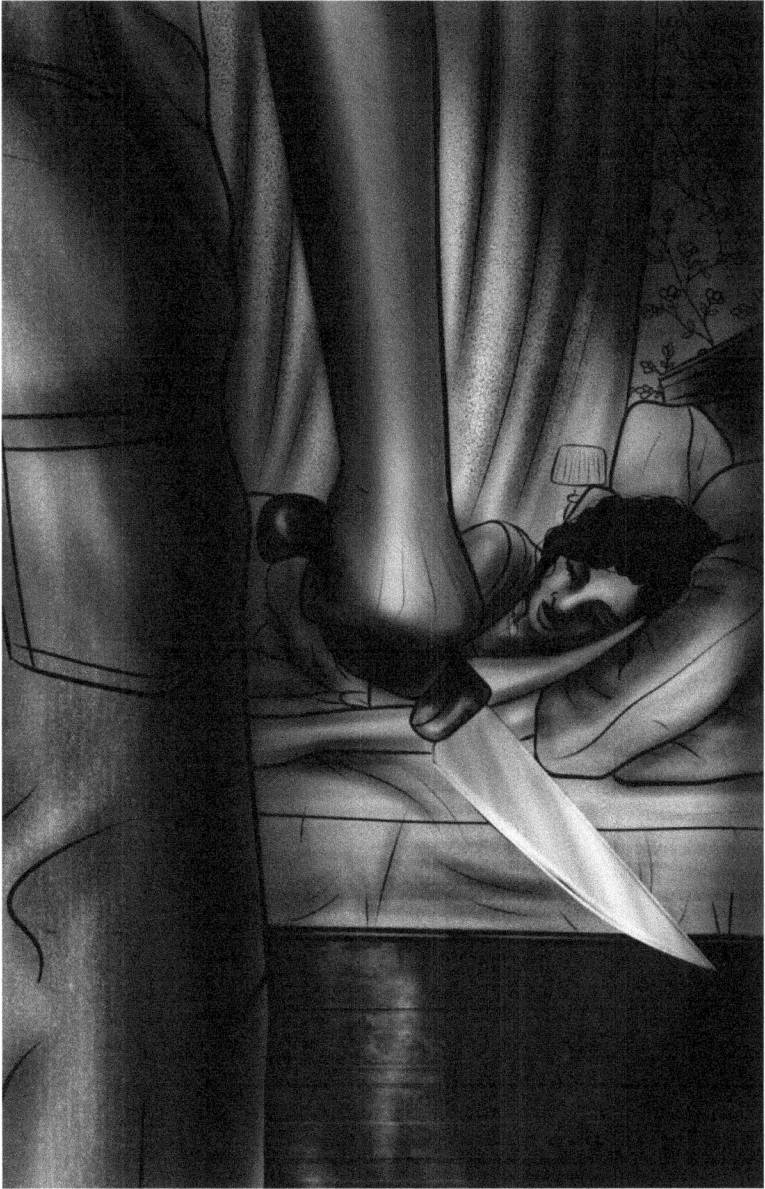

Startled by the sudden lights, he turned around and when he saw my grandmother, he quickly hid the knife behind his back. Grandma enraged, started yelling at him, screaming to get away from her daughter.

Mom woke up, startled, and saw the knife. She started crying in fear at the sight of what was in his hand, which only meant one thing he was going to kill her. "Don't you dare ever lay another hand on my daughter or my granddaughters!" *"No te atrevas mas nunca a ponerle una mano encima a mi hija o a mis nietas!"* she exclaimed.

He carefully placed the knife on the night table, while he tried to explain to abuela the reason he held a knife in his hands over my mother while sleeping. Needless to say, my grandmother did not believe a word he said.

I remember the next morning there were two extra people in our beds, Mom and Grandma. The door had a chair propped against the doorknob, and there was a bat and knife next to our beds.

Unsurprisingly, the ogre had so many apologies lined up before he left to work. He pleaded his case from outside the barricaded door of our bedroom.

Mom and Grandma listened out to hear him leave. Once they heard his loud work bus leave, we knew he would be gone for at least eight hours.

We exited our room, ate breakfast, and were sent to the living room to play with our dolls while they spoke in the kitchen. They spoke for a while; I even heard them make phone calls. At the time, I couldn't understand what in the world was going on with those two. Yet, even with everything going on, they made sure to make a feast for us to eat for dinner.

One thing I couldn't wrap my head around to was: why my grandma was still there? She did not look the other way like everyone else had. Could it be … could she be the answer to my prayers to God? Did He hear me and send her to save us? Grandma had no fear on her face, none at all. Mom, on the other hand, I could tell she was nervous.

The feast was one to remember. I thought to myself: *wow this is what the table set up looked like!* The menu included Spanish rice, baked chicken, beans, standard salad and potato salad, among other things.

All too soon, we heard the loud bus arrive. The ogre made it back home. His bus had a very distinguishing sound it made, like tree nuts were rattling in the muffler.

Once he opened the front door, I'm sure he did not know what to expect. Us children were sitting on the living room floor and Grandma was sitting down on the sofa watching TV while we played. My mom was waiting for him in the kitchen. She was acting normal, back to her usual routine with him once he arrived, as if my grandma were not there.

He had a stunned face once he saw Grandma in the living room—she did not look at him at all as he entered. Mom continued to tend to him—she helped take off his jacket as he sat down. Then she took off his boots and socks.

The bathroom was right across from the kitchen, so he went right in there to take a shower, Mom followed him. My mom helped him shower, and once done, went to the kitchen to serve his food.

He sat down in the dining room, still confused as to why my grandmother was still there. Everyone was still very quiet; it was so awkward. Once we all finished our dinner, we returned to what we were previously doing.

He had his special recliner seat in the living room that he went to with a beer in his hand. I didn't know what to expect from anyone in that room. I was just as confused as he was. I suspected my mother and grandmother were up to something, I just couldn't figure it out at the time. But I went on to do what I was instructed to do, which was to keep my sisters busy.

Finally, the silence broke, he faced Grandma and said, "Mother-in-law, forgive me. I would never hurt your daughter, believe me when I say I love her," which in Spanish was, *"Suegra perdoneme. Yo nunca le haria daño a su hija, creame cuando le digo que la amo."*

Grandma only replied with, "Just remember what I told you last night, don't ever forget that." *"Solo recuerda lo que te dije anoche, que nunca se te olvide."*

That was the first time ever seeing that man put his head down, as a sign of respect towards my grandmother, it was so unbelievable.

Go Grandma!

For the next two days, everything at the house seemed weirdly quiet, as if nothing bad had ever happened.

Chapter 16: Getaway

My grandmother left to go back to Puerto Rico on the third day, the ogre even gave her a big hug before leaving, I could tell he was so happy.

On day four and five, oddly enough, we were still living in a dream. There was no screaming, no objects being thrown, no belts being used to hit us, no hurting my mom. Was I dreaming? It was like I was; I couldn't believe it. It was... too good to be true.

Day six arrived, and the ogre was particularly jubilant at the start of the work week, so it had to have been a Monday. My mom followed her normal morning routine with him. She made sure everything was done for him before he left for work.

As the ogre left the apartment and drove away something different happened. Mom's body language shifted, she had a sense of desperation in her facial expression. When she reached the window to see him go, she called me over to her by the sofa. As I stood next to her, she asked me to stay and keep watch for the work bus.

She instructed me to remain at that window. We had to confirm that the bus was not turning back.

As soon as his work bus made the turn to get out of the block, I had to let her know he had left. While we were waiting for the big bus to disappear, she was scrambling all around the apartment looking for something. Once I couldn't see that bus anymore, I shouted out to her that he was gone. She ran to the window, started to wave at someone outside in desperate motions. Something was definitely up.

She turned to me and placed both of her hands on my shoulders and tells me *"Esto es importante, ve y despierta tus hermanas y calladitas,"* in English, "This is important, go and wake up your sisters and be quiet."

I saw Mom run to her room, so I ran to my room to wake up my sisters. I saw the desperation in my mom's actions, so I knew whatever was happening was supposed to happen. I was not going to question or hesitate for anything. She started to pull luggage out from under the bed and from the laundry room. Now that everyone was up and alert, Mom says to me, "Just put on your sneakers, there is no time to change," in Spanish, *"Ponte las tenis, no hay tiempo para cambiarse."* I couldn't understand why we were about to leave in pajamas, but I did not care. I realized it was going to be another attempt to escape.

Suddenly, someone starts knocking at our door. My sisters and I jumped, afraid of what was beyond the door. Mom passed us to open the door; it was my mom's three teenage nephews. They said to my mom as soon as she opened the door, "Hurry, hurry. His bus is long gone but we got to be fast about this before he suspects something and returns."

My sisters, not understanding what was going on, were nervous. They started to cry because they did not want to leave their dolls. They wailed about being hungry as well. I remember my sister Mirla still being a toddler needed her bottle.

My cousins helped my mom get the luggage down the stairs to the person waiting for us on the 1st floor; my mom's sister, my aunt with worry creases between her eyebrows. She apologized to my mom for not helping sooner. My aunt told her that she loved her and continued to tell her that everything was going to be ok as she hugged her. She turned to us, kissed all of us on our foreheads, and said her goodbye's.

My mom's nephews called us all over to a black limousine. At nine years old and in the late 80's, I knew that was the coolest thing ever to be in a limo. Despite the circumstances, I felt like a super star, I was so excited about riding in what any other day would have been luxury. One of the joys of those agonizing years for me was that limo ride.

We were all in our pajamas, sneakers, hair a mess, only carrying one doll or stuffed animal, bottles of milk and about four medium suitcases. That was it, we had to leave 80% of our belongings behind at the apartment.

I can still see the fear in my mom's face as we drove off, she kept looking behind us to make sure the ogre wasn't following us. She hoped he hadn't figured anything out. It wasn't until we made it to the airport, got out of the limo, and went into the waiting area that my mom looked calm— I mean even the color in her face was returning. I even heard a sigh of relief once we were on the airplane.

Second amazing thing was being on an airplane, flying to an unknown destination.

I was aware that we were fleeing, but I was clueless about where we were going.

All I knew was this time the mission was going to be complete, there was no turning back after this. Eventually all the adrenaline and excitement left our bodies, and we all fell asleep on the airplane ride. Excited but scared at the same time, I wondered if we were leaving for better or for worse.

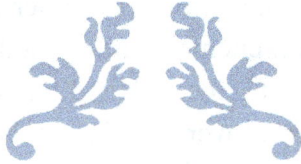

Chapter 17: The Light At The End Of The Tunnel

O nce we arrived at our destination, we exited the plane and at the entrance of the airport was our ride. One of my mom's brothers, our uncle whom we never met before, was standing there waiting for us. I can still remember his big smile. I could see how happy he was to see us. He immediately hugged my mom and got down on his knee to embrace my sisters and I. From my height, he looked as tall as a giant.

Turns out, my mom has four brothers—three older and one that was younger than her, all of whom lived in Puerto Rico and we had not met yet.

I remember the car ride being so long, but I also remember seeing all the beautiful views of the mountains, the beaches. The people also looked so different, so humble. As I looked out the window, the air was blowing in my face and it felt so good, I felt so free.

At that moment our spirits, once weighed down like heavy
stones, now floated like feathers on the breeze. However, I

still had a very small, unsettling feeling that I couldn't ignore.

I thought to myself, was this it? Did we finally escape? But the most important question of them all, will he find us? And if he does, what will he do to us? The fear of uncertainty was there; it couldn't be helped.

Be aware that the mind of a nine-year-old girl is filled with these thoughts. Someone, despite the distance, still instilled a sense of fear in me. Therefore, if I experienced such feelings, I could only speculate on what my mother perceived and how it affected her emotions.

We finally arrived at our destination, Villalba, Puerto Rico. We got out of the car, and I remember seeing trees all around. Before I realized it, a few children approached us, embraced us, and in English introduced themselves as our cousins.

I felt a surge of excitement as I began to experience a hint of love; I felt accepted rather than rejected.

As we went down this small unpaved hill, a man approached me, kneeled down in front of me and said to me "I am one your uncles so don't be scared, my name is Tio Roman you are safe, and no one can hurt you here. I promise." I wrapped my arms so tightly around his neck and started to cry. "Thank you," I said. He picked me up and placed me over his shoulder, grabbed my mom and pulled her in for a hug. My sisters were being carried by my other uncles.

He kept walking down the rest of the small unpaved hill where we could see a house with more people waiting for us.

All my little cousins were running down the hill and the others were walking next to us.

My mom reached the house first; her other sisters and sisters-in-law were there waiting for us with arms wide open. They hugged my mom so tight, almost like they didn't want to let go. There were tears of joy everywhere I looked. Everything about my environment changed, so suddenly and unexpectedly, I had the impression that things would keep getting better.

While on my uncle's shoulders, I extended my arms to the side, closed my eyes, took a deep breath of the fresh air around me. It felt so good. The sun was shining through the tree branches with the wind blowing gracefully as it brushed along my face.

I could hear animals around me, and when I turned to see where the sound was coming from, I could see them.

It was the first time I ever saw chickens with their little ones. Butterflies had so many beautiful colors. There was even a peacock. As it spread its feathers and displayed those amazing bright colors, it took my breath away. The elegance and freedom in the way it displayed its feathers was stunning.

Was I dreaming? There was no way I was dreaming. It felt like at any moment it could be taken away, like when I was younger, and my imagination only lasted so long before reality came crashing back. As I was being carried, I strayed from reality for a few minutes. I started to compare my imaginary world to the world I was really in. I could picture the whole tribe of mermaids and fairies as the big family in front of me that I was not aware of. The lake and the fields of color in Arstenia were all the beautiful nature that surround me.

As the breeze flowed through the branches, the trees seemed to sigh with contentment, sharing the joy of freedom with every gentle rustle. The King and Queen represented my grandma and mom, whom I saw as my protectors. But the best part of all was, there was no sign of any ogres.

I *already* felt so loved there, and my sisters as well, they looked so excited with everyone and everything that was around them. This was a new experience for us. It was as if we were imprisoned for years, and we were finally let out of our confinement. As my uncle placed me back on the ground to walk, I noticed this one familiar face coming out of the house.

I recognized that long, beautiful, black, shiny hair, and that light cinnamon color skin! I ran as fast as I could to hug her; it was my grandmother! She hugged me and told me how much she loved us, and how happy she was that we were finally there with her.

I started to say to myself at one point *"Could it be? Did He really hear me? Did He somehow have something to do with Grandma showing up to help us?"* You know? God, the one Mom would talk to every night asking for help. All I know is that Grandma sought answers to inquiries regarding our wellbeing, and what better method to find out, than to visit and observe for herself.

Did He persuade her to go on that trip in order to find the answers she sought? Of course He did! I think I got my answers too once I saw her there at that moment. She was our guardian angel, a shield of light that dispelled the shadows of doubt and fear that once surrounded us. I am eternally grateful to her, and everyone else involved for saving our lives.

She was worried about her young one, and her motherly instinct pushed her to find out about her daughters and granddaughters wellbeing.

We were safe, I was finally safe! A new life awaited us in our new home, and we were ready to discover it with no fear holding us back.

One more time I turned to look at everything that surrounded me at that moment. As the sunlight flickered on my skin, the light just seemed to laugh, as if celebrating my newfound happiness and the beginning of a joyful chapter.

Looking over the mountains I noticed a rainbow. It looked so beautiful and peaceful. The colors sang in harmony, each note echoing a promise that we would pave a path to freedom together.

Epilogue

"SAFE"

Afro fter arriving at our destination, Puerto Rico life
became simpler for us (by simpler I mean very
humble). Once we spent time with the family, we
headed up to my grandmother's house where we were about
to embark on a journey that showed us how some families
truly cohabitate. The drive was scary and exciting at times.
There were so many up and down hills, at times you looked
to the side, and you could see cliffs. So many tiny houses,
people outside sitting hanging out drinking what I assumed
was coffee. A lot of animals everywhere we looked; dogs,
chickens, cows, goats etc.... There were many trees and
vegetation around us as we headed to Grandmother's house.
The sun was shining so bright, it reminded me of a huge light
bulb in the sky.

Once we arrived, we exited the car and approached this gated
property. Inside this property was a very tiny blue wooden
house. We went up the steps, headed inside the home, the
living room was small, it had one sofa with a knitted blanket
on it. My grandmother then showed us her bedroom and
proceeded to lead us to what would be our room for slumber.
There was one big bed, I believe it was full-size, and next to
it was a twin bed.

We then headed over to the kitchen. I remember there were
some shelves with pots on the wall. The sink just sat on a
long sheet of wood, with all the piping showing at the
bottom. There were no kitchen cabinets, no stove. Outside
there was a very small hut, with pots and pans hanging on
the outside. On the counter there was a lot of ash as if stuff
was burned there. When I asked my grandmother what it

was, she told me it was her outdoor stove. It was where she prepared all the food.

She then proceeded to walk over to this tiny, tiny shed. As she opened the door, this horrendous smell overwhelmed my senses. As my sisters and I pinched our noses; I asked what that was. "Your bathroom," she replied with a smile. I looked at her, and then I looked over at my mom and couldn't believe that was true. It was something I have never seen before as a child, a flat raised surface with a hole in the middle (the toilet). It's called an outhouse with a pit latrine.

I was honestly horrified by the site of it, my little sisters as well. She then went over to the side of the outhouse where there was an outside shower. It had some raised wooden planks high enough to cover an adult up to the height of the neck and low enough where you could only see the person's feet. The shower head was a hose tied up to the wall and just hanging there to be used when we showered.

We then walked down this little path further back from the house, where we heard many different noises. It turns out my grandmother had a chicken coop. There were chickens everywhere. Now that was very exciting to see. I had never seen a chicken in person, they were running all around the property, trying to fly away from us as we tried to catch one of them.

My little sisters were having so much fun just chasing them. They all had different colors for their feathers, brown, black, white, and red. The rooster, however, had lovely colors in his feathers, black with a shiny dark blue glare on them with some red streaks. We also got to pick the eggs from the chicken's nest. As we continued the tour around my grandmother's property, I could only stare in awe at all the beauty mother nature had to offer. It still reminds me of the fairy world that I dreamt of.

I could see on my mother's face. She was relieved. She had such a big smile it was like she was starting over again in life. *Finally*. We got the help we needed.

It seemed God truly had listened, and he answered our prayers. At last, we were all safe.

Facts About Domestic Violence

Facts about Domestic Violence from the 1970's till the present day:

In 1970 domestic violence was ignored and unrecognized by the legal, medical and social domains. Police and medical professionals were hesitant to intervene in such cases when they were present. A husband beating a wife was considered a "private matter."

Women movements soon started to gain momentum. Advocating awareness, policy changes, and survivor support became their goal.

First Shelters for battered women became active in the late 60's and early 70's.

Restraining orders were first implemented in the 1970's.

The legal system was slow-moving in addressing domestic violence, and protection orders were not strictly enforced.

"We will not be Beaten" became the slogan for The Battered Women's Movement. They advocated for change and support.

Services soon started to emerge by 1971, starting with the first emergency rape crisis line in Washington, DC. After that the first hotline for battered women began in 1972, in Minnesota.

By 1978, more than 170 women shelters opened across the country.

In 1978, The National Coalition Against Domestic Violence was founded to advocate for change.

(*circulatingnow.nlm.nih.gov*)

In the 1980's

By 1983, over 700 domestic abuse shelters were operating in the United States. They provided shelter and support to women.

In 1984, President Ronald Reagan signed the Victims of Crime Act (VOCA) into law, establishing the Crime Victims Fund.

In 1985, the Surgeon General workshop on Violence and Public health finally recognized Domestic Violence as a public health problem. In doing so, health professionals, law enforcement, social services, and psychology were educated on the approach to address the violence.

Regardless of these developments, domestic violence continued to be a prevalent issue, with numerous victims encountering institutional obstacles in their pursuit of justice and assistance.

By 1989, the United States operated 1,200 programs for battered women, providing shelter for 300,000 women and children annually.

(*www.cawc.org/news/things-to-know-about-the-history-of-the-domestic-violence-movement*

Pennsylvania Child Welfare Resource Center

American Medical Association)

In the 1990's

In 1990, for the first time judges were required to consider any history of spousal abuse before determining child custody or visitation rights.

The American Medical Association issued guidelines in 1992, recommending that physicians assess women for indicators of domestic violence.

The Surgeon General identified spousal abuse as the primary cause of injuries among women aged 15 to 44, according to a report from 1992.

In the 1990s, the United States experienced a reduction in domestic violence, as the incidence of intimate partner violence fell by 64%, from 1994 to 2010. Additionally, the Violence Against Women Act (VAWA) was enacted in 1994, to address and prevent gender-based violence.

The United States enacted the Violence Against Women Act, recognizing domestic violence and sexual assault as criminal offenses in 1994, which was signed by President Bill Clinton.

VAWA created acknowledgment and assistance for shelters addressing domestic violence, rape crisis centers, and various community organizations dedicated to eradicating domestic violence across the country.

(www.pacwrc.pitt.edu

https://bjs.ojp.gov/content/pub/pdf/ipv01.pdf

www.thehotline.org)

On February 21, 1996, the National Domestic Violence Hotline answered its very first call.

Present Day, every 9 seconds in the U.S., a woman is assaulted or beaten. Every year, 1 in 3 women who is a victim of homicide is murdered by her current or former partner.

On a typical day, domestic violence hotlines nationwide receive approximately 20,800 calls.

15.5 million children witness domestic violence each year.

Domestic violence accounts for 15% of all violent crimes.

Domestic violence is most common among women ages 18-24 and 25-34.

Only about half of intimate partner physical violence is reported to law enforcement.

(https://www.thehotline.org/about/history-of-the-hotline/

www.safehomesdv.org/Domestic-Violence-Statistics)

What is Domestic Abuse?

Domestic abuse refers to any effort by one individual in a marriage or intimate partnership to exert power and control over the other person.

An abuser employs tactics such as fear, guilt, shame, and intimidation to undermine an individual and maintain dominance over them.

It can happen to anyone; but almost always they target the weak minded. Although women are more frequently targeted, men also endure abuse.

Domestic abuse frequently progresses from intimidation and verbal attacks to physical violence.

Although physical harm may represent the most apparent threat, the emotional and psychological effects of domestic abuse are equally significant.

Abusive conduct is always intolerable; we have the right to feel appreciated, respected, and secure.

What are some of the signs of an abusive relationship?

If you find yourself needing to tread carefully in their presence—constantly monitoring your words and actions to prevent an outburst—it's likely that your relationship is unhealthy and abusive.

If you are not sure, talk to a professional. Or refer to the information at the end of the book.

Does your partner belittle or raise their voice at you?

If your partner frequently criticizes you, belittles you, mistreats you to the point of embarrassment, or even holds you responsible for their own abusive actions, it is an indication that your relationship is unhealthy.

Violent behavior?

If your partner exhibits an erratic temper that leads to physical harm or threats to your life, you are in an abusive relationship.

Alternative methods they might display as aggressive behavior include threatening to remove your children from your care or even inflicting harm upon them.

Exhibiting extreme jealousy, possessiveness, or attempting to control your movements and activities is a significant warning sign of an abusive relationship.

If your partner restricts your interactions with family and friends, controls your access to finances, the internet, phone, and vehicle, it indicates that you are in an unhealthy relationship.

Disregarding those indicators could result in life-threatening consequences.

Physical and sexual abuse

Physical abuse takes place when force is applied to you in a manner that causes harm or poses a threat to your safety or that of your children.

Physical assault constitutes a criminal offense, and law enforcement has the power and authority to safeguard you against such attacks.

Victims often choose to remain in abusive situations, driven by fear of potential consequences from their partner.

Sexual Abuse

Any circumstance that compels you to engage in non-consensual or humiliating sexual acts constitutes sexual abuse.

Sexual coercion, regardless of whether it is perpetrated by a spouse or intimate partner with whom one also engages in consensual sexual activity, constitutes an act of aggression and domestic violence.

Additionally, individuals whose partners inflict physical and sexual abuse upon them face an increased likelihood of sustaining severe injuries or even losing their lives.

Recognizing the warning signs of abuse

Even though you won't know exactly what happens behind closed doors, you can look for warning signs if you suspect domestic abuse. Don't ignore these warning signs if you see them in a friend, family member, or coworker.

Here are some signs to look for:

1. Appear apprehensive or nervous about pleasing their partner.
2. Comply with their partner's actions and words.
3. Receive frequent, harassing phone calls from their partner.
4. Discuss their partner's possessiveness, jealousy, or anger.
5. Sustains injuries on a regular basis while claiming that it was an accident.
6. Frequently skips social events, work, or school without giving a reason.
7. Always wear clothes that cover up scars or bruises, especially in warm weather.
8. Be prohibited from seeing friends and family.

Final Notes from the Author

Please speak up if you suspect domestic violence or abuse. Talk to the person in private and let them know that you are concerned. Make sure they know you are there for them when ready to talk.

Are you telling yourself that it is none of your business? You may be mistaken and taking no action could further damage that person's life.

Remember that voicing your worries will show the person that you care and are concerned about them; in doing so you could potentially save their life.

Thank you.

Sincerely,

Jen Torres

Daughter, Mother, Wife, Friend, and Author.

Helplines and support.

Help for women.

In the U.S.

National Domestic Violence Hotline

For anonymous, confidential help 24/7

1-800-799-7233

Visit **https://www.thehotline.org/**

Canada

Visit **https://sheltersafe.ca/**

UK

Visit **www.womensaid.org.uk/**

Ireland

Visit **www.womensaid.ie/**

Australia

Visit **https://1800respect.org.au/**

Help for men.

In the U.S. and Canada

Call the National Domestic Violence Hotline

1-800-799-7233.

UK

Visit **https://mankind.org.uk/help-for-victims/**

Ireland

Visit **https://www.mensaid.ie/amen-is-now-mens-aid-ireland/**

Australia

Visit **https://www.oneinthree.com.au/**

www.ingramcontent.com/pod-product-compliance
Lightning Source LLC
Chambersburg PA
CBHW071952100426
42736CB00043B/2969